AN ARTIST ON THE EASTERN FRONT
FELIKS TOPOLSKI 1941

CONTRIBUTORS

Laura Brandon, Nicolae Harsanyi, Jon Mogul

Kara Pickman, editor
Marlene Tosca, art director
Tim Hossler, designer
David Almeida and Lynton Gardiner, photographers

The Wolfsonian–Florida International University
1001 Washington Avenue
Miami Beach, FL 33139
wolfsonian.org

The Wolfsonian receives ongoing support from the John S. and James L. Knight Foundation; State of Florida, Department of State, Division of Cultural Affairs and the Florida Council on Arts and Culture; Miami-Dade County Department of Cultural Affairs and the Cultural Affairs Council, the Miami-Dade County Mayor and Board of County Commissioners; and City of Miami Beach, Cultural Affairs Program, Cultural Arts Council.

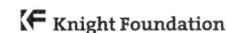

Knight Foundation   MIAMIBEACH

Cover image: Feliks Topolski, Untitled, 1941. Pen, ink, and graphite on paper, 10 3/4 x 14 3/4 in. (27.3 x 37.5 cm). The Wolfsonian–FIU, Gift of Jean S. and Frederic A. Sharf, 2013.17.1

Published by The Wolfsonian–Florida International University, Miami Beach, on the occasion of the exhibition *An Artist on the Eastern Front: Feliks Topolski, 1941*, opening November 21, 2015.

© 2015 Florida International University Board of Trustees

All rights reserved. No part of this book may be reproduced or utilized in any form or by any means, electronic or mechanical, including photocopying, recording, or by any information or retrieval system, without permission from the copyright holders.

Printed and bound in the United States by Shapco, Minneapolis
First edition

ISBN: 978-0-9968699-0-4

Library of Congress Cataloging-in-Publication Data

Names: Topolski, Feliks, 1907-1989. | Brandon, Laura, 1951- | Mogul, Jonathan, 1963- | Harsanyi, Nicolae
Title: An artist on the Eastern Front : Feliks Topolski, 1941
Includes bibliographical references.
Identifiers: LCCN 2015038380 | ISBN 9780996869904 (alkaline paper)
Subjects: LCSH: World War, 1939-1945--Soviet Union--Pictorial works. | World War, 1939-1945--Art and the war. | Poland. Armia--History--World War, 1939-1945--Pictorial works. | World War, 1939-1945--Social aspects--Soviet Union--Pictorial works. | Soviet Union--Social life and customs--1917-1970--Pictorial works | Topolski, Feliks, 1907-1989--Travel--Soviet Union. | Soviet Union--Description and travel.
Classification: LCC D764 .T665 2015 | DDC 940.53/47--dc23
LC record available at http://lccn.loc.gov/2015038380

CONTENTS

4   FOREWORD
       Timothy Rodgers

7   COLLECTOR'S MESSAGE
       Frederic A. Sharf

8   FELIKS TOPOLSKI, 1907–1989
       Jon Mogul

11   FELIKS TOPOLSKI, WAR ARTIST
       Laura Brandon

19   PLATES
       Texts by Nicolae Harsanyi

FOREWORD

Timothy Rodgers

Director, The Wolfsonian–Florida International University

Feliks Topolski is not a household name, even among art lovers. If you go to London, his adopted hometown, and you want to see his work, you might skip the city's great museums and head straight for the bar that bears his name. But if Topolski has not been fully recognized in the canon of great twentieth-century artists, he certainly belongs in the canon of great artistic witnesses to the events of the century. The sketches on view in *An Artist on the Eastern Front: Feliks Topolski, 1941*—scenes from the Soviet Union during its darkest hour in the Second World War—are just a small part of a body of work that spanned decades and continents.

Topolski's drawings clearly belong at The Wolfsonian–Florida International University, with our mandate to collect and interpret the visual and material artifacts of the modern era. For that reason, when Jean S. and Frederic A. Sharf approached the museum in 2013 with the offer to donate fifty-six of Topolski's drawings from his time in the Soviet Union, as well as related books and magazines, we were delighted to accept. This book and the exhibition it accompanies are the results of that gift and of the Sharfs' generous financial support.

This project is the latest in a series that has only been made possible thanks to the Sharfs' ongoing contributions. Few collectors have a keener appreciation for the Wolfsonian's mission than Fred Sharf, and few allies of the museum have shown as strong a commitment to helping us build our collections. Fred has brought us not only Topolski, but also a wealth of other collection material, ranging from automotive design drawings to photograph albums made by colonial officials to chromolithographs from the Spanish-American War. The Wolfsonian's library has benefited especially from the Sharfs' support, which has both expanded its holdings and provided the resources we need so that our cataloging can keep pace as the boxes of books and albums have come in.

I want to give my deepest thanks to Jean and Fred for sharing the fruits of their resourceful collecting with The Wolfsonian and with our community. My sincere thanks also go to art historian and curator Laura Brandon, of Carleton University and the Canadian War Museum, Ottowa, whose essay on Topolski in the context of British war art has greatly enriched this book, and to my many colleagues at The Wolfsonian for their diligent work in realizing an exhibition and book of this caliber.

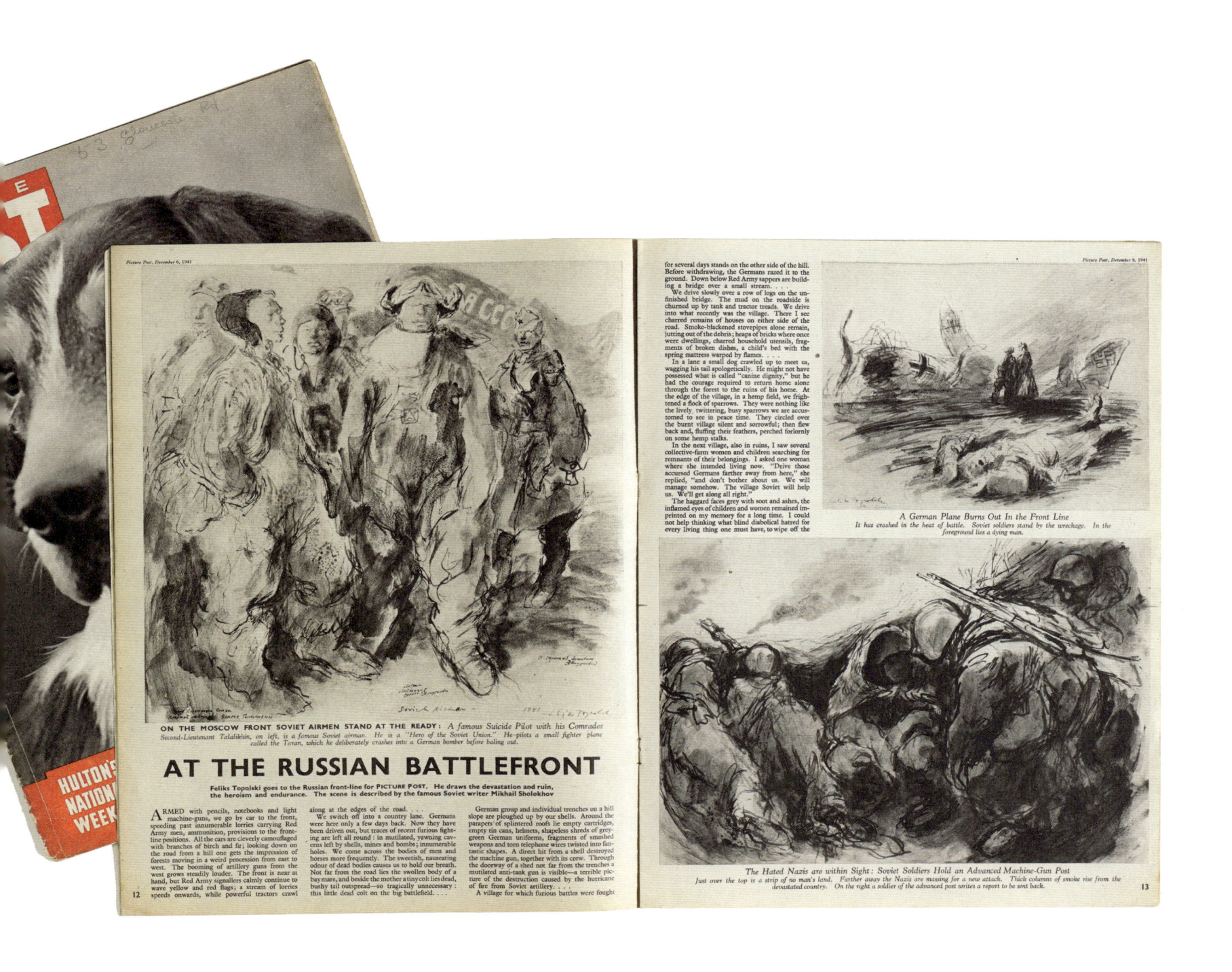

Illustrations, 1941. Feliks Topolski. From *Picture Post*, December 6, 1941, 12–13. [Background: *Picture Post*, November 29, 1941.] 13 3/4 x 10 1/4 in. (35 x 26 cm). The Wolfsonian–FIU, Gift of Jean S. and Frederic A. Sharf. XC2013.11.8.9–10

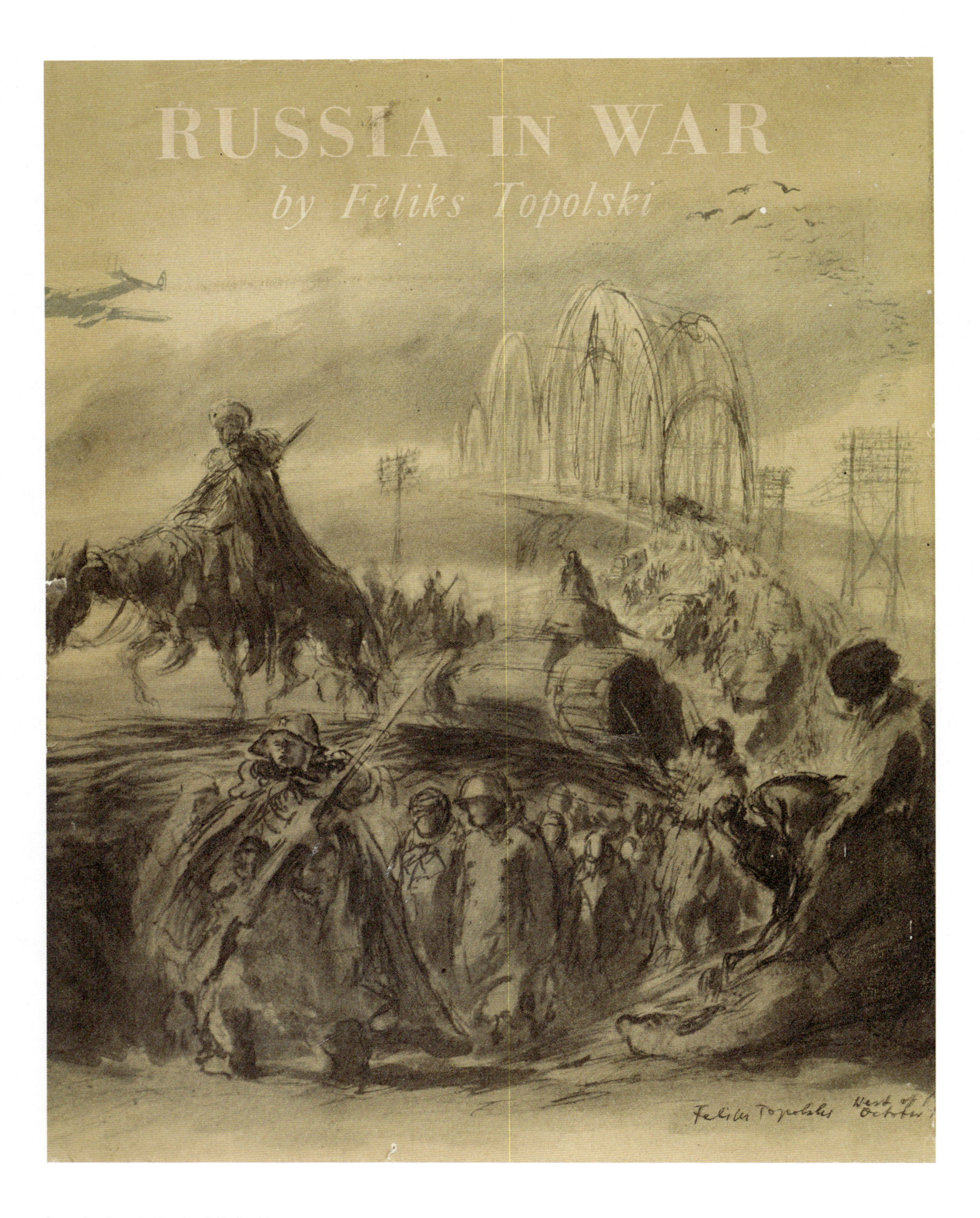

Dust jacket, *Russia in War*, 1942. Feliks Topolski,
illustrator. Methuen & Co. Ltd, London, publisher.
12 1/2 x 10 1/4 in. (32 x 26 cm). The Wolfsonian–FIU,
Gift of Jean S. and Frederic A. Sharf, XC2013.10.25

COLLECTOR'S MESSAGE
Frederic A. Sharf

Feliks Topolski first came to my attention in 2010. I was collecting British wartime propaganda scarves at the time and occasionally acquired scarves that featured imagery from Topolski's drawings. I was attracted to the artist's unique style.

Early in 2012, my London business associate Leslie Verrinder received a phone call from Teresa Topolski, the artist's daughter. She wanted to sell her father's leather wardrobe trunk, which had been custom made for him in India. Leslie bought the trunk, restored it, and sold it to me in October of that year.

That transaction opened a line of communication to Teresa, and I asked Leslie to find out whether she had any drawings by her father that she would be willing to sell, particularly from the war years, 1939 to 1945. Teresa invited Leslie and me to meet her for coffee at the Topolski family house, where she still lived, on Saturday, November 10, 2012. I decided that my best chance to strike a deal lay in concentrating on a single aspect of Topolski's wartime work—his 1941 trip to Russia.

Teresa was in the process of selling the family house and moving to an apartment at the time. We agreed to meet again, together with her brother Daniel Topolski, in February 2013. For that meeting, Teresa and Daniel had assembled all the drawings from their father's 1941 trip to Russia for me to examine. While many were no longer in good condition, I felt the drawings told an important story, and we agreed on a price. Leslie housed the works in acid-free Mylar sleeves and sent them to my office, where Angel Morales spent months conducting research to assemble the full story of Topolski's journey to Russia.

Once the story was fleshed out, I knew that the perfect home for the drawings was The Wolfsonian–Florida International University. I had promised the Topolski family that the drawings would not be sold or broken up, and that my wife Jean and I would donate them to an appropriate American institution—and I kept my promise!

FELIKS TOPOLSKI, 1907–1989

Jon Mogul

Assistant Director for Research and Academic Initiatives,
The Wolfsonian–Florida International University

"Kick the door open—the hum of life turns into a roar. All of humanity is out there." These words, quoted from a 1946 magazine article, give an impression of how Feliks Topolski viewed his art and his life.[1] The London Blitz; Moscow under German assault; and Second World War campaigns in the Middle East, South Asia, and Italy; the liberation of the Bergen-Belsen concentration camp; the return of displaced persons after the war, the Nuremberg trials, India's independence, and Vietnam; the Cultural Revolution in China and the civil rights movement in the United States—this roll call of momentous events and deadly conflicts may read like the resumé of a Magnum photojournalist, but it in fact describes (and only partly) the settings for thousands of scenes that Topolski witnessed and sketched on paper.

Topolski, who lived most of his life in London and became a naturalized British citizen in 1947, was born and raised in Poland to Jewish parents, who converted soon after his birth. He studied at the Warsaw School of Fine Arts and also served in the Polish artillery. As a student, he had illustrations published in the satirical weekly *Cyrulik Warszawski* (Warsaw Barber), and later became a prolific contributor to a number of Polish periodicals. In 1935 he traveled to Britain for a Polish literary periodical to record scenes from King George V's silver jubilee. Perhaps sensing the growing threats to Poland's security, lodged as it was between Adolf Hitler's Germany and Joseph Stalin's Soviet Union, he remained in London after finishing his assignment.[2]

Topolski was immediately enamored of London, and of British life in general, as Laura Brandon notes in her essay in this book. The British public took to Topolski as well. He published his drawings from the jubilee in the book *London Spectacle 1935* in his first year there, during which time he also exhibited his work at the Wertheim Gallery, earning praise from the *Times*. Soon he was contributing frequently to American and British publications ranging from *Harper's Bazaar* to *Night and Day* and *Studio*. During this period he also began a collaboration with George Bernard Shaw, providing

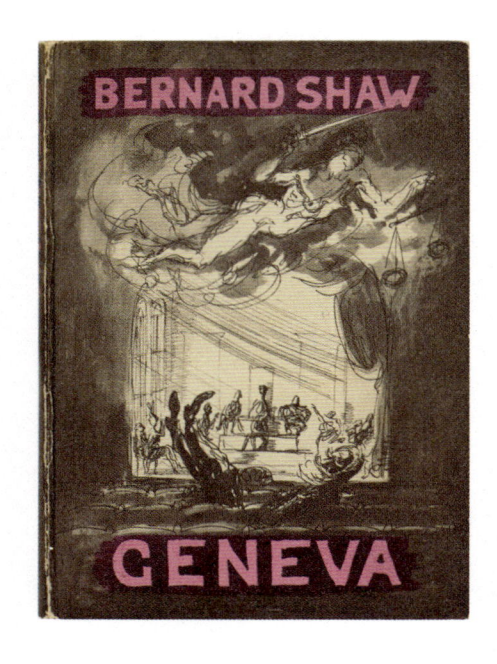

Fig. 1
Book cover, *Geneva*, 1939. George Bernard Shaw, author. Feliks Topolski, illustrator. Constable & Co., London, publisher. 7 7/8 x 6 in. (20 x 15 cm). The Wolfsonian–FIU. Gift of Jean S. and Frederic A. Sharf. XC2013.11.8.1

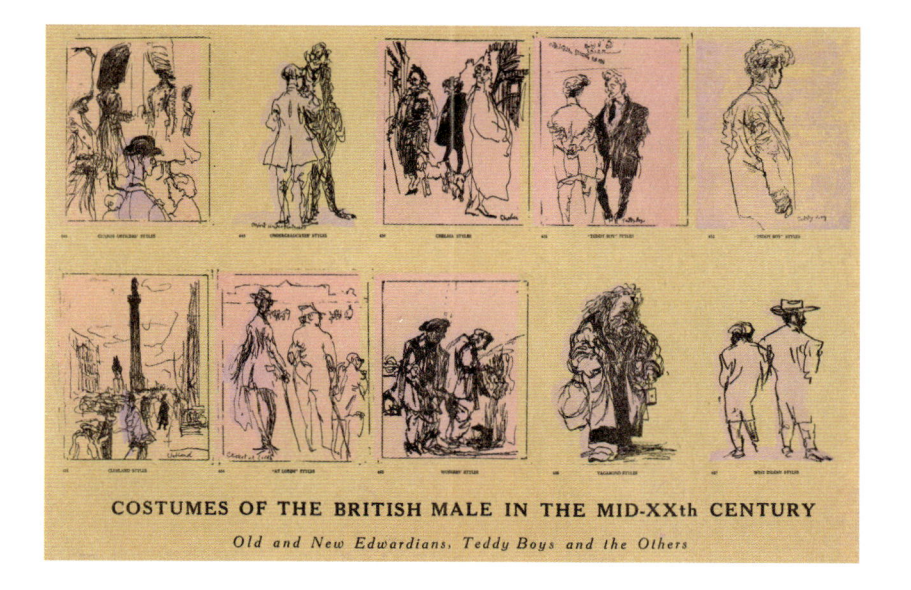

Fig. 2
Illustrations, "Costumes of the British Male in the Mid-XXth Century," 1954. Feliks Topolski. *Topolski's Chronicle* 3, no. 8: 44. 18 1/8 x 11 3/4 in. (46 x 30 cm). The Wolfsonian–FIU, Gift of Jean S. and Frederic A. Sharf, XC2013.11.8.17

illustrations for the publication of Shaw's plays *Geneva* (1939, fig. 1) and *In Good King Charles's Golden Days* (1940).[3]

Shaw returned the favor (somewhat bombastically) by calling Topolski "perhaps the greatest of all the Impressionists in black and white," in a blurb for the artist's 1941 book *Britain in Peace and War*.[4] His account of his 1941 visit to the Soviet Union, *Russia in War*, followed the next year, while *Three Continents 1944–45*, which included scenes from the Mediterranean, the Middle East, South Asia, China, and, finally, the Allied campaign in Italy, appeared in 1946. Together with London exhibitions and periodicals that featured many of the same drawings, these books made Topolski's version of the world war familiar to a mass public in Britain. A *Life* magazine feature in 1945 claimed that "probably no artist has seen so much of this war as Feliks Topolski."[5]

Topolski was no less busy after the war, when he established himself in a studio beneath the arch of the Hungerford Bridge, near Waterloo Station in London's South Bank neighborhood. His work for magazines took him to the inauguration of the United Nations and the Nuremberg trials; he "reported" on the end of the British Raj and India's independence, and on insurgencies in French Indochina, Malaysia, and Northern Ireland; he went to China during the Cultural Revolution, and Chicago during the 1968 Democratic Convention. He returned to Moscow for the 1969 May Day parade—the drawings he made of the occasion were featured in a film produced by CBS News.[6]

Although his work continued to feature in mass media, Topolski also launched a remarkable self-publishing venture in 1953. *Topolski's Chronicle* was a biweekly broadsheet, hand-printed on cheap paper using a press in his studio, that was sold on the street and sent by subscription to individuals and libraries (and, according to the artist's son Daniel, to the White House) (figs. 2–3).

The *Chronicle*, printed in editions of two thousand, showed the full range of the artist's interests: street scenes he observed in London and in his travels all around the world, sketches showing contemporary fashions, and portraits of personages from Winston Churchill to Jawaharlal Nehru to Malcolm X to Elvis Presley. The actress Joyce Carey called it "the most brilliant record we have of the contemporary scene as seized by the contemporary mind."[7] For Topolski, the *Chronicle* offered a "rough and ready" means to bring the products of his ceaseless drawing into the public sphere:

> Drawings of genre, of life, need a platform: it's no use scribbling on and on and just tucking the results away in corners. In the old days there were broadsheets and prints, but modern newspapers are not enough. They grudge you space and I was in need of a vehicle for my continuity. The *Chronicle* was started against advice and without capital, but it supported itself from the beginning.[8]

Topolski owed his reputation and his popularity to his drawings. He did complete two prominent, large-scale painting projects, however. In 1959 he was invited to paint a series of panoramas for a corridor in Buckingham Palace, depicting long processions of British people entering and leaving Westminster Abbey for Queen Elizabeth II's 1953 coronation. In 1975 he began a project that he would call *Memoir of the Twentieth Century* (or *Memoir of the Century*), in the arches under the Hungerford Bridge. *Memoir* became a six-hundred-foot-long painted account of the great events of his time, beginning with the Blitz and reproducing many of the scenes that he had captured in his drawings over the decades.[9]

Feliks Topolski died at age 82, on August 24, 1989. His studio under the Hungerford Bridge arch is now a bar, called Topolski, where patrons can view many of the paintings that made up *Memoir*.

Fig. 3
Illustrations, "The State Visit of an African Monarch" (top) and "Sunday Piccadilly Circus," 1956.
Feliks Topolski. *Topolski's Chronicle* 4, no.13–14: 73–74.
18 1/8 x 11 3/4 in. (46 x 30 cm). The Wolfsonian–FIU,
Gift of Jean S. and Frederic A. Sharf, XC2013.11.8.17

[1] The article appeared in *Listener*. Quoted in Bernard Denver, "The Eye of History: The Art of Feliks Topolski," in *Topolski's Buckingham Palace Panoramas* (London: Quartet Books, 1977), 6.
[2] James Laver, "Feliks Topolski," in *Britain in Peace and War*, 2nd ed. (London: Methuen & Co., 1946), 4–7; "Feliks Topolski," *Times* (London), August 25, 1989.
[3] Laver, "Feliks Topolski," 7; Feliks Topolski with Peter Ford, "Collage," in *Topolski's Buckingham Palace Panoramas*, 12–16; "Christmas Art Shows," *Times* (London), December 14, 1935.
[4] Display advertisement for *Britain in Peace and War*, *Times* (London), November 7, 1941.
[5] "Polish Artist Sketches the War All the Way around the World," *Life*, March 19, 1945.
[6] Topolski and Ford, "Collage," 22–24; Daniel Topolski, "Feliks Topolski: Eye Witness to the 20th Century" (lecture, Museum of London, March 22, 2010). http://www.gresham.ac.uk/lectures-and-events/feliks-topolski-eye-witness-to-the-20th-century.
[7] Denver, "The Eye of History," 5.
[8] "Topolski's Chronicle," *Times* (London), March 16, 1959.
[9] Information about *Memoir* can be found at the website Topolski Century, http://www.topolskicentury.org.uk/memoir/. See also Richard Morrison, "Secret Story," *Times* (London), May 17, 2008.

FELIKS TOPOLSKI, WAR ARTIST

Laura Brandon

Adjunct Research Professor, Carleton University, Ottawa

Research Associate, Canadian War Museum, Ottawa

Fig. 1
Poster, *Paul Nash, An Official Artist on the Western Front*, 1918. Paul Nash (British, 1889–1946), designer. Vincent Brooks Day and Son, London, printer. Offset lithograph. 30 1/8 x 20 1/8 in. (76.5 x 51.1 cm). The Wolfsonian–FIU, The Mitchell Wolfson, Jr. Collection, TD1991.143.2

In the aftermath of the First World War, the art produced during the conflict proved to be as significant for forging national identities as it was for visually documenting each country's experience of battle. In Britain and Canada, for example, the quality of the artists employed and the art they produced helped set benchmarks for each country's postwar national schools. In Canada, there would have been no Group of Seven without the conflict, and in Britain, the wartime work of artists such as Paul Nash and Stanley Spencer, to name just two, established new and significant aesthetic standards (fig. 1). When the Second World War broke out, Sir Kenneth Clark, the youthful director of London's National Gallery, swiftly proposed a second British war art scheme. Partly inspired by the Depression-era American Federal Art Project,[1] Clark wished to protect British artists' lives and the country's freshly invigorated school of art from decimation.[2]

One artist who held a somewhat ambiguous position with respect to Clark's aims for the war art program was Feliks Topolski. From 1935, when he moved to England from Poland and launched his successful career as an illustrator and caricaturist, Topolski's superior sketching skills were well-recognized and appreciated by artists and commissioning agencies alike. Before, during, and after the war, he had easy access to the high and mighty and to the lowly and frightened, and his pencil and pen were constantly at work. He loved the theatricality of traditional rituals that he found in Britain, and he treasured military pomp, all of which aided opportunity and acceptance in his own time.

Likely unseen for decades, in a National Gallery of Canada file of printed ephemera belonging to the Canadian war artist Carl Fellman Schaefer (1903–1995), is a folder marked simply "Topolski," which offers some evidence of the high public regard he enjoyed just after the war. Inside the folder are two articles Schaefer clipped from immediate postwar editions of American *Vogue* and *American Artist*.[3] *American Artist* provides us with a piece of self-promotion presented in the form of an illustrated summary of Topolski's career, from his birth in Warsaw, his art

Fig. 2
Dust jacket, *Britain in Peace and War*, 1946 (first published 1941). Feliks Topolski, illustrator. Methuen & Co. Ltd, London, publisher. 12 1/2 x 10 1/4 in. (32 x 26 cm). The Wolfsonian–FIU, Gift of Jean S. and Frederic A. Sharf, XC2013.11.8.2

school training, his burgeoning career as a magazine illustrator and muralist, his military experience, his move to England (he became a naturalized citizen in 1947), his drawings of King George V's silver jubilee, and his work as a globe-trotting war artist,[5] primarily in his official capacity with the Polish government-in-exile, to a successful New York exhibition of his war work in 1945, and, finally, to the announcement of the "recent" publication of his book *Britain in Peace and War* (actually first published in 1941), from which the article's illustrations derive (fig. 2).

The *Vogue* article is interesting for reasons that have less to do with self-promotion. Shortly after North Korea invaded South Korea in 1950 and the United States sent troops to support South Korea in July, Topolski was in Washington, DC, and able to sketch direct and indirect responses to recent events in a variety of ways, from a portrait of Senator Robert A. Taft speaking in the Senate to a scene of still-wounded Second World War veterans convalescing at Walter Reed General Hospital. Other portraits introduce us to the members of the Supreme Court, the upper echelons of the US Air Force, and a number of high-flyers in Washington society. Sixty-five years after the fact, Topolski's lively portrait sketches still put us in the moment, demonstrating the skill that is central to any understanding of his earlier Second World War work, whether it is scenes of fear or frivolity in bomb shelters (while sketching in 1941, Topolski himself was badly injured in an air raid), war-devastated London homes, or, as viewed in this exhibition, the Russian experience of the German invasion in 1941.

These clippings (and also, perhaps, the fact that Schaefer bothered to save them) evidence Topolski's reputation in the postwar years as an exemplary draftsman and as an important artist. During the war itself, his graphite and ink and wash drawings of London and Russia were published and circulated around the world in books with introductions written by important figures.[6] Nevertheless, Topolski gets barely a mention in Brian Foss's magisterial 2007 work on the British Second World War art program *War Paint: Art, War, State and Identity in Britain 1939–1945* or in Monica Bohm-Duchen's 2013 detailed survey *Art and the Second World War*.[7] One reason for the scant attention from historians concerned with war art is that, for all his wartime popularity and recognition in Britain, Topolski never became a full-time salaried war artist with the official War Artists' Advisory Committee (WAAC), receiving only a single short-term contract to make air-raid drawings in 1940 (he also sold some work to the committee).[8] The small role he played in the government's official art campaign is, itself, likely connected to an ingrained, if unacknowledged, prejudice against commercial art on the part of the WAAC, which favored an art for art's sake model. Clark, who ran the WAAC, viewed it as a nurturing institution for British art and, indeed, Britishness. Clark's favorite artists were Henry Moore (1898–1986), Paul Nash (1889–1946), John Piper (1903–1992), and Graham Sutherland (1903–1980), all of whom produced work in a particularly British idiom that in Clark's opinion marked them as different from the French or German schools.[9]

Clark did admire Topolski's skills and accommodated him in the British artist pantheon by placing his work in the context of the great British tradition of humorous art.[10] Positioned within the framework of such historic practitioners of the art of caricature as George Cruikshank (1792–1878), James Gillray (1757–1815), and Thomas Rowlandson (1756/57–1827), Topolski's work could be elevated above mere illustration. It is interesting that Clark never mentioned the resemblance between Topolski's work and that of graphic artist Honoré Daumier (1808–1879), particularly their shared use of chiaroscuro (or contrasts of dark and light) for dramatic effect. *Manicure Booth at the Grand Hotel—Kuibyshev* (pl. 10) shows Topolski's utilization of this approach to good effect. A hotel manicurist works on a client's hands and nails in a brightly lit cubicle surrounded by shadowy figures whose indistinctness emphasizes her particular concentration. Clark's nation-building exercise, however, had no place for French graphic precedents. What mattered was national identity. If Topolski's art could be integrated into a British tradition, its foreign influences and origins could be overlooked, if not buried.

Despite Clark's high regard for his skill, correspondence between the WAAC and Topolski in the files of the Imperial War Museums suggests that the committee's support had significant limits, primarily in terms of purchasing, which Topolski clearly resented. Clark preferred to promote Edward Ardizzone (1900–1979), another illustrator, albeit one who worked more often in color, and, despite his Italian name, captured successfully the particularly British sensibility that Clark admired. Thus when Topolski went to Russia in 1941, it was not under the auspices of the WAAC, but

Fig. 3
Illustration, "West of Moscow. October 1941," 1941. Feliks Topolski, illustrator. Frontispiece to *Russia in War*, 1942. Methuen & Co. Ltd, London, publisher. 12 1/2 x 15 5/8 in. (32 x 40 cm). The Wolfsonian–FIU, Gift of Jean S. and Frederic A. Sharf, XC2013.10.25

rather under a commission from the Polish government-in-exile, which had moved from Paris to London the previous year.

Topolski, as he wrote in *Russia in War* (1942), "went to Russia as a member of the Polish diplomatic mission and as a Polish officer" (fig. 3).[11] He also describes himself ambiguously as an envoy of the British war art program (which he was not; his 1940 commission was finished) and as a London *Picture Post* correspondent. That he went at all is surprising, since Poland had a less-than-happy relationship with Russia, especially in the wake of the Soviet invasion of Poland in 1939 and the subsequent Katyn massacre in 1940, in which an estimated twenty-two thousand Poles were killed. Topolski, however, recognized the British fascination with the country's wartime Soviet ally, and knew that the opportunity was his to capitalize on, as the WAAC did not acquire much work concerning the Soviet Union.[12] (Indeed Foss does not document any official attempt to do so, nor is there evidence of such work in the Imperial War Museums' art collections other than the limited purchases from Topolski mentioned above.)

Curiously, despite his clear responsibility to witness, Topolski wrote, "I over-filled my bag of experience, yet my sketch-books contain only a few notes." He tactfully explained that he found it difficult to have the "freedom to draw and a great part of my work was done later from memory."[13] There is, however, so much work from his time in the Soviet Union that one wonders whether his memory was assisted by photography in some way. As is the case with many artists of this time, any resort to the photographic tool is rarely mentioned.[14] Although his personal use of a camera would have been strictly limited, he may have had access to Soviet-produced images, useful in the depiction of landmarks like the

Kremlin, for example. *Red Square, Moscow* (pl. 14) may be an example of a scene that drew on photography. Like many of his drawings involving architectural scenes, the human elements—the military parade, individual soldiers, as well as vehicles—seem somewhat awkwardly incorporated. The clearly recognizable buildings look a little like stage sets against which a generic humanity plays out its various wartime roles. This conclusion is supported by Topolski's own remarks in *Russia in War* when he compared the Soviet experience with what he had recently witnessed in the streets of London in 1941. "I was flooded with associations," he writes, "it had all happened before."[15] This comment perhaps explains why he ultimately described his work as more about composition than detail.[16]

While in the Soviet Union in September and October 1941, Topolski spent time in Moscow and traveled east to visit Polish army camps as a member of the Polish diplomatic mission. Judging by the dates on his drawings, he was barely there a month. But his output was prolific and, if not sketched on the spot, his work certainly was completed close to the time he was there. The strength of this work lies primarily in the portraits. Those included in *Russia in War* and in this exhibition evidence an artist who was sympathetic to the varied experiences of people in conflict situations. *Shoe Cleaner, Moscow* (pl. 21), a swiftly rendered ink and wash drawing, depicts an elderly shoe cleaner huddled near a sandbagged Moscow wall. *Moscow* (pl. 18) captures in wash and a few expressive ink lines a small group of warmly wrapped elderly Muscovites walking along a street. Set against a sparsely delineated group of more brightly lit seated figures, *Moscow Metro* (pl. 17) contrasts the dark form of an elderly man asleep in the shadows of a Moscow subway station that is his shelter against German bombing raids. Although Topolski does not exclude other war experiences—an illustration published in *Russia in War* shows a prison camp, for example (fig. 4)—the strongest pictures draw on memories of his London experiences of the Blitz, a subject he had recently lived through and sketched in an official capacity, and an experience that clearly still haunted him. A comparison between his 1940 London Tube and shelter sketches published in *Britain in Peace and War* (fig. 5) and his published Moscow Metro sketches in *Russia in War* makes this abundantly clear (pl. 17). For all Topolski's Polish background and position and his encounters with Polish soldiers in the Soviet Union, he had no direct experience of

Fig. 4
Illustration. "A Prisoner's Camp." 1941. Feliks Topolski. From *Russia in War*, 1942. Methuen & Co. Ltd, London, publisher. The Wolfsonian–FIU, Gift of Jean S. and Frederic A. Sharf, XC2013.10.25

Fig. 5
Illustration. "The Tube, Autumn 1940," 1940. Feliks Topolski. From *Britain in Peace and War*, 1946 (first published 1941). Methuen & Co. Ltd, London, publisher. 12 1/2 x 10 1/4 in. (32 x 26 cm). The Wolfsonian–FIU, Gift of Jean S. and Frederic A. Sharf, XC2013.11.8.2

Poland's recent history. In 1941, by then six years a resident of Britain, he was channeling the Soviet experience of war at least as much through British as through Polish eyes.

Topolski's work during his mission to the Soviet Union in 1941 raises a number of interesting questions. This essay has already addressed the circumstances of Topolski's wartime commissions, his subject matter, and the artist's approach to his work. Another issue centers on the reception of Topolski's art in the context of war and, in the longer view, his wartime work's reputation in the British war art canon and British art as a whole—a reputation that was affected by two facts: that Topolski was Polish by birth rather than British, and that he was best known as a commercial illustrator and as a caricaturist. Before, during, and after the war, the English-speaking public appreciated his drawings in magazines and books for the shared international human experiences they captured, but they were not primarily the stuff of art gallery exhibitions except during the conflict itself, when in the context of a depressed wartime art market, Topolski's broadly popular work presented an irresistible opportunity for commercial galleries.[17] The response was not always critically positive. When Topolski's Russian work was exhibited in 1942 at Thomas Agnew & Sons in London, influential critic Eric Newton drew attention to its resemblance to "fantasies" rather than "the documentary statements of an eye-witness."[18] This called into question the degree of direct observation Topolski employed in his Soviet assignment. Newton's final put-down was to describe Topolski's work as "un-English." Comments such as these helped further diminish any canonical future for his war work in the postwar British roll call Clark so assiduously cultivated, an omission this exhibition seeks to address.

[1] Kenneth Clark to Humbert Wolfe (Ministry of Labour deputy secretary), October 3, 1939, National Gallery Archive, London, Central Register for Artists in Wartime (1939), quoted in Brian Foss, *War Paint: Art, War, State and Identity in Britain, 1939–1945* (New Haven, CT: Yale University Press; London: Paul Mellon Centre for Studies in British Art, 2007), 19.

[2] Kenneth Clark, *The Other Half: A Self-Portrait* (London: John Murray, 1977), 22.

[3] Printed ephemera related to the Library of Carl Fellman Schaefer, Ottawa, National Gallery of Canada Archives, SCS1 SCHA4 P75.

[4] "In Washington: Sketched for *Vogue* by Feliks Topolski," *Vogue*, August 1, 1950, 55–58; "Feliks Topolski," *American Artist*, March 1948, 26–29.

[5] Topolski documented his wider travels in Feliks Topolski, *Three Continents, 1944–45: England, Mediterranean Convoy, Egypt, East Africa, Palestine, Lebanon, Syria, Iraq, India, Burma Front, China, Italian Campaign, Germany Defeated* (London: Methuen & Co. Ltd., 1946).

[6] *Russia in War* (1942) contains an introduction by Sir Richard Stafford Cripps, the British ambassador in Moscow in 1941. James Laver, the Victoria and Albert Museum in London's then Keeper of Prints, Drawings, and Paintings, contributed to *Britain in Peace and War* (1941).

[7] Monica Bohm-Duchen, *Art and the Second World War* (Farnham: Lund Humphries, 2013), 43, 210 (a US edition was published by Princeton University Press in 2014).

[8] The correspondence on Topolski's relationship with the WAAC is in the artist files of the Imperial War Museums, London. ART/WA2/03/101. http://www.iwm.org.uk/collections/item/object/1050000881.

[9] Clark's emphasis on the British qualities of war art is noted in a review of an exhibition he curated for the Museum of Modern Art, New York. Edward Alden Jewell, "Artists Depict a War-Torn World," *New York Times*, June 1, 1941.

[10] Foss, *War Paint*, 165.

[11] Feliks Topolski, *Russia in War* (London: Methuen & Co. Ltd., 1942), 9.

[12] Foss, *War Paint*, 118.

[13] Topolski, *Russia in War*, 10.

[14] Of relevant interest is recent scholarship suggesting that, despite contrary statements from the artist, a number of Henry Moore's wartime shelter drawings were based on published photographs. See, for example, Roya Nikkhah, "Henry Moore 'Copied Drawings from Magazine,'" *Daily Telegraph*, February 20, 2010, http://www.telegraph.co.uk/culture/art/art-news/7277843/Henry-Moore-copied-drawings-from-magazine.html.

[15] Topolski, *Russia in War*, 7.

[16] Ibid., 10.

[17] Foss, *War Paint*, 183.

[18] Eric Newton, "Topolski's Russia," *Sunday Times*, August 9, 1942.

Many of the drawings reproduced here were published in Feliks Topolski's book *Russia in War* (1942) under slightly different titles than those he inscribed on the drawings themselves. Where there is a significant discrepancy between the two, or where no title appears on the drawing, the title given in *Russia in War* is shown in brackets.

All drawings were made during Topolski's visit to Russia in September and October 1941. Dates are given only when Topolski indicated the particular month on the drawing.

All works are from The Wolfsonian–FIU, Gift of Jean S. and Frederic A. Sharf.

PLATES

FELIKS TOPOLSKI, DRAWINGS FROM RUSSIA, 1941

Texts by Nicolae Harsanyi, Associate Librarian, The Wolfsonian–Florida International University

20

PLATE 1

[*Aboard the* Llanstephan Castle]

Pen, brush, ink, and graphite on paper
9 1/2 x 11 7/8 in. (24.1 x 30.1 cm)
2013.17.38

SS *Llanstephan Castle* was an ocean liner requisitioned by the British government from Union Castle Lines to join the first British convoy that shipped military materials to the Soviet Union after the Nazi invasion of June 1941. The convoy wound its way through the Arctic Ocean to the port of Arkhangelsk in northern Russia. Feliks Topolski sailed among the civilian passengers on board *Llanstephan Castle* as a commissioned war artist for the Polish government-in-exile, based in London. At the same time, Topolski was under contract with the magazine *Picture Post*, which published many of his drawings after his return to London in late October 1941. The speed with which Topolski executed sketches made him an ideal witness to the Allied military convoy and the mission to set up an army of former Polish prisoners of war to fight against the Germans. This drawing shows a British officer saluting a destroyer that accompanied and protected the convoy.

PLATE 2

Untitled

Pen and ink on paper
8 3/4 x 5 3/4 in. (22.2 x 14.6 cm)
2013.17.27

Topolski found himself in the USSR at a moment of military crisis. The German offensive that began in summer 1941 had captured much of European Russia by the time he arrived in September, and now an assault on Moscow was about to begin. He recorded many scenes of military and civilian life both inside and outside the Soviet capital. Since authorities did not permit foreign citizens to take photographs, these sketches stand as an invaluable visual document of the Soviet Union during those weeks when its fate hung in the balance.

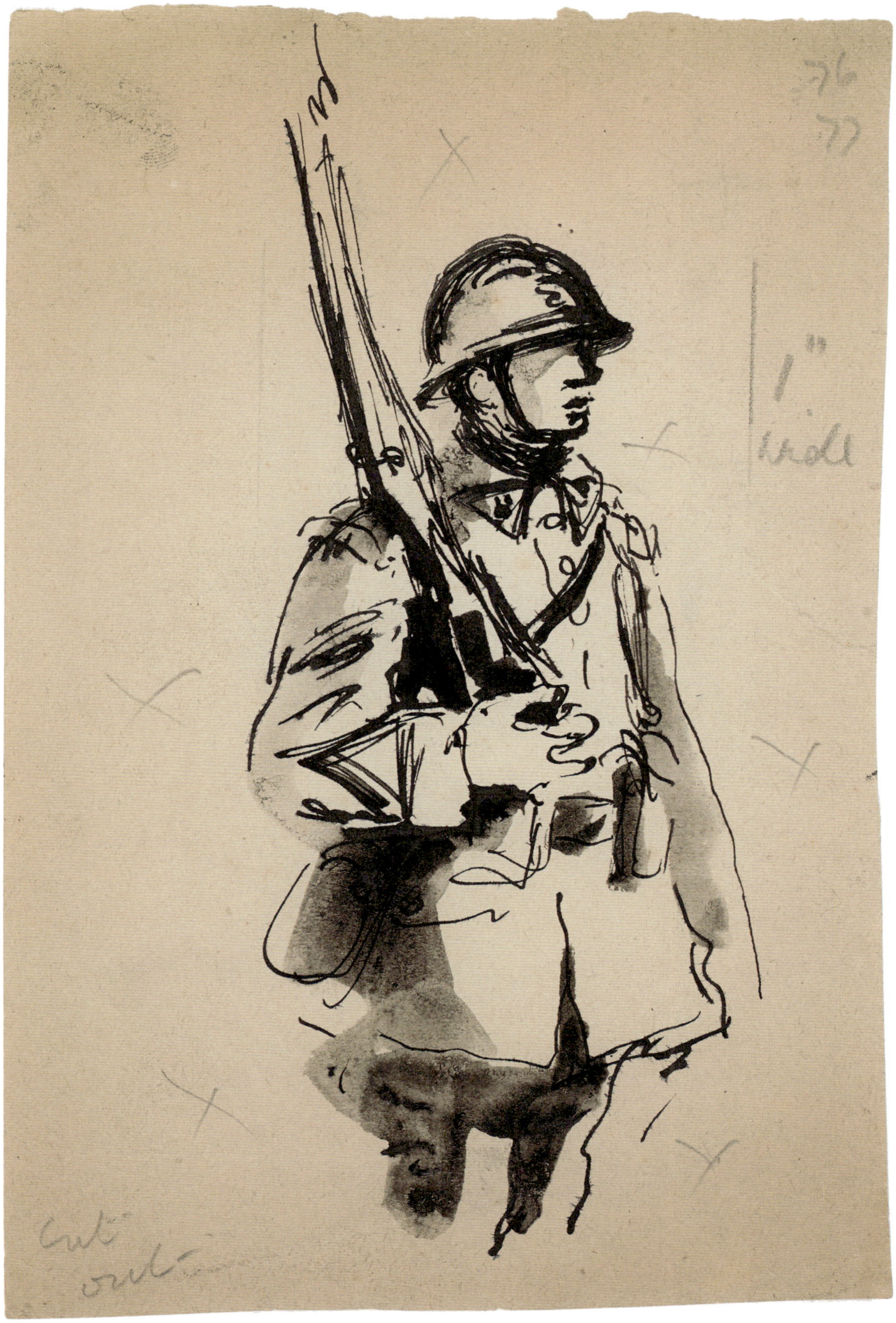
76
77
1" wide
Cut out

medical corps nurses of a "Komsomol druzina"

PLATE 3

Medical Corps Nurses
[*Front-line Nurses*]

Pen, brush, and ink on paper
8 1/4 x 10 5/8 in. (21 x 27 cm)
2013.17.32

Along with millions of men, thousands of women served at the front in 1941, including in combat units. In the early months of the war they wore men's uniforms. The nurse depicted here, in the center, is wrapped in a rain-repellent cape that could also serve as a tent cover.

PLATE 4

Untitled

Pen and ink on paper
6 3/4 x 5 1/4 in. (17.1 x 13.3 cm)
2013.17.26

Dressed in full combat gear, an officer and a soldier hurriedly stride forward, while a T-34 tank and a fighter plane can be seen in the background. Foot soldiers were expected to cover up to twenty-five miles in a day. Officers were issued shielded caps and leather boots, while enlisted soldiers wore forage caps on their heads. When the Second World War engulfed the Soviet Union in 1941, Moscow had the largest army in Europe, with almost two million soldiers. The disadvantage of this immense force was the expense of clothing such numbers, so Soviet troops entered the conflict in dress designed under the tsarist regime in the early 1900s.

PLATE 5

Peasants

Pen, brush, and ink on paper
8 1/4 x 10 5/8 in. (21 x 27 cm)
2013.17.32

This drawing, along with several similar scenes, appeared on a page titled *Refugees in the Station Square* in Topolski's book *Russia in War* (1942). The figures in the drawing may have been rural people who fled parts of the western Soviet Union that had been conquered by the Germans for safer territory near the Ural Mountains.

PLATE 6

Indecipherable title

Pen and ink on paper
5 1/2 x 7 in. (14 x 17.8 cm)
2013.17.42

Late 1941 saw the creation of the Polish Army in the Soviet Union. This force was made up of some of the more than 1.5 million Poles who were deported to forced labor camps throughout the Soviet Union after the Nazi and Soviet invasions of Poland in 1939. After two years of languishing in the Lubianka prison in Moscow, General Władysław Anders was set free and tasked by the Polish government-in-exile to organize this army. Equipped with uniforms and boots provided by the British government, the Polish fighters started to train to face the enemy, but lack of food, weapons, and medical supplies prompted General Anders to take the army out of the Soviet Union via Iran in 1942. Subsequently this army of seventy-five thousand men, also known as Anders' Army, fought alongside the Western Allies in Italy and on other European fronts. General Anders is second from left in this group of Polish officers.

PLATE 7

Day Nursery

Pen, ink, watercolor, and graphite on paper
5 1/2 x 7 in. (14 x 17.8 cm)
2013.17.35

Topolski here depicts a scene in the countryside, set on a collective farm, or kolkhoz. Such farms had been established by the Communist authorities in order to merge small family farms into large enterprises and achieve state control over agriculture. After the October Revolution in 1917, most churches, such as the one shown here, were converted to secular use, often housing schools, movie theaters, or administrative offices. The five-pointed star, a symbol of the revolution, dominates the entrance to the premises of the collective farm; Topolski ironically juxtaposed it to the crosses atop the church's onion domes.

PLATE 8

Buzuluk—Local Soviet

Ink on paper
5 1/2 x 7 in. (14 x 17.8 cm)
2013.17.19

Buzuluk is a town in southeastern European Russia, situated at the south end of the Ural Mountains. There Topolski visited a camp for Polish prisoners of war that had been transformed into a training camp for the Polish Army in Russia. The image shows a room of the local administration (known as a *soviet*). A portrait of Joseph Stalin hangs on the far wall.

PLATE 9

Village Market

Ink and watercolor on paper
5 1/2 x 7 in. (14 x 17.8 cm)
2013.17.25

Topolski shows women selling produce displayed in stalls in the background of this market scene. In the foreground, with his coat worn as a mantle, an officer stands in front of a soldier. The blue collar patches indicate that he serves in the forces of the People's Commissariat for Internal Affairs, or NKVD. The five-pointed star on his belt buckle is replicated by the red star on the forearm of his uniform. The third five-pointed star on the officer's chest was a decoration for military service.

PLATE 10

Manicure Booth at the Grand Hotel—Kuibyshev

Pen, brush, and ink on paper
5 1/2 x 7 in. (14 x 17.8 cm)
2013.17.20

Kuibyshev (now Samara) is a large city in the southeastern part of European Russia on the east bank of the Volga River. During the Second World War, Kuibyshev was chosen to be the capital of the Soviet Union should Moscow fall to the invading Germans. In October 1941, with the Germans approaching Moscow, the Communist Party and governmental organizations, diplomatic missions of foreign countries, and leading cultural establishments were all evacuated to the city. Topolski traveled by train to Kuibyshev on his way to Buzuluk.

PLATE 11

Archangel
[*Archangel in the Snow*]

October 1941
Ink on paper
5 1/2 x 6 7/8 in. (14 x 17.4 cm)
2013.17.36

The northern Russian city of Arkhangelsk lies on the banks of the Dvina River near its exit into the White Sea. During the war, the city became known in the West as one of the two main destinations (along with Murmansk) for the Arctic Convoys bringing supplies to assist the Soviet war effort. Topolski sketched this street scene in October, as he was about to depart for England, after the first snow had already fallen. The building in the center of the picture is made of logs, a typical construction material in heavily forested northern Russia, and has a food store (*gastronom*) on the first floor. The sign on the adjacent building identifies it as a movie theater. Various forms of transportation can be seen on the roadway, including a streetcar, a horse-drawn wagon, and an automobile.

35

PLATE 12

[*A German Bomber*]

October 1941
Graphite and ink wash on paper
12 15/16 x 15 13/16 in. (32.9 x 40.2 cm)
2013.17.34

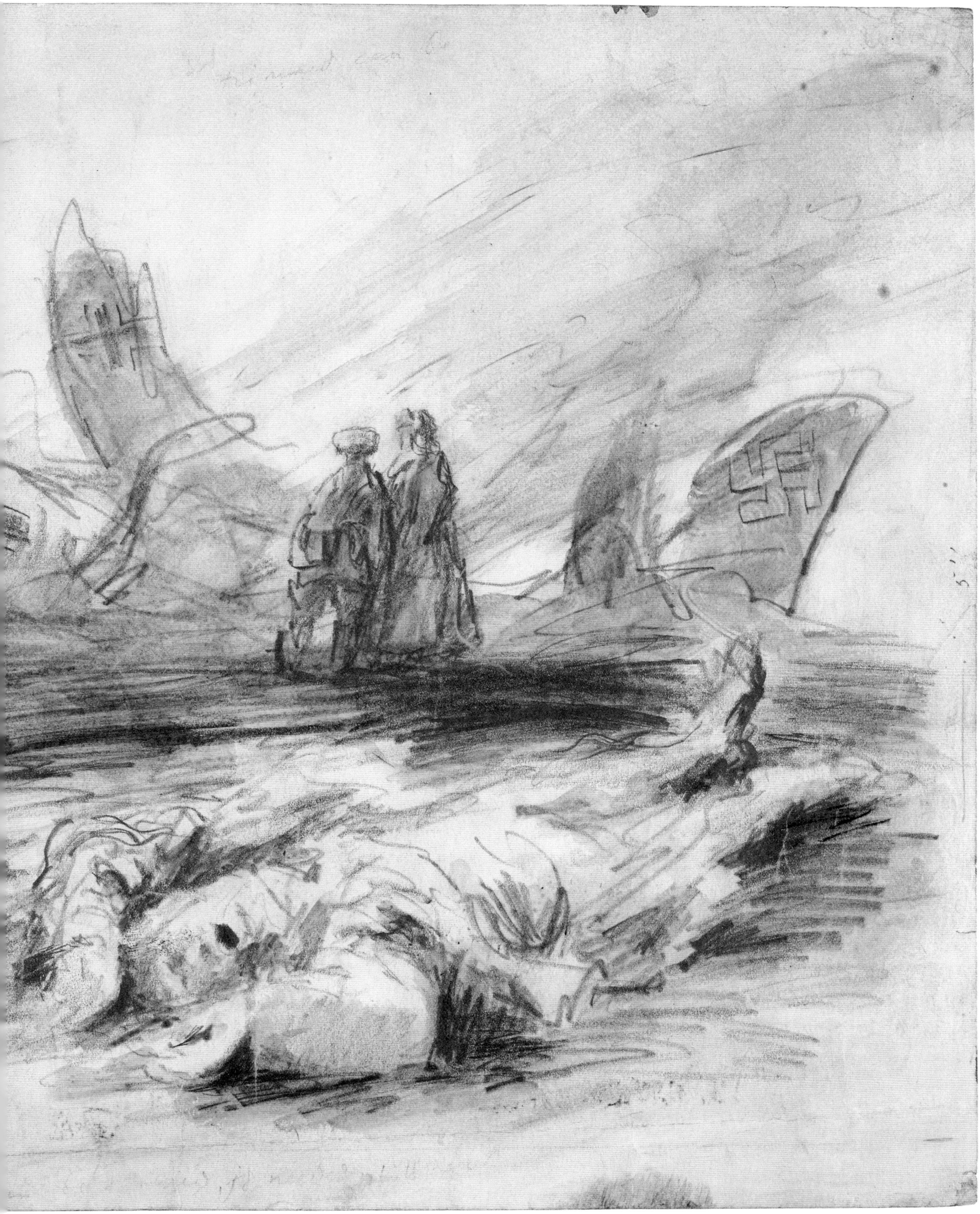

PLATE 13

*A Student Girl on Night Duty
at the University during an Air Raid*

Brush and graphite on paper
12 3/8 x 9 5/8 in. (31.4 x 24.4 cm)
2013.17.13b

Women, whether workers or students, were recruited to perform civil defense duties at their factories or universities. Here Topolski sketched a young woman wearing overalls and a gas mask, holding a sign that reads *zarazheno* (infected), which was intended to mark spots that were impacted in a chemical weapon attack. The Soviet Union, like other governments, prepared its soldiers and civilians to defend against chemical weapons, which both sides had used during the First World War. Despite these fears, chemical weapons were not used on either the eastern or western fronts during the Second World War.

ЗАРАЖЕНО

triangle to be put
over infected spot
during gas attack

5 7/8

Член местной
команды по охране
здания

Д.П.
1941 Ipril

A student girl on night duty at the University during an air-raid.

PLATE 14

Red Square, Moscow
[*St. Basil's Cathedral*]

September 1941
Ink and graphite on paper
7 1/4 x 9 13/16 in. (18.4 x 24.9 cm)
2013.17.2

A well-known view of Moscow's Red Square is dominated by Saint Basil's Cathedral. Topolski shows columns of troops marching in front of the cathedral, across the square. Although Adolf Hitler planned to conquer Moscow in the first months of the war, the German invaders were stopped outside the city limits. The farthest German advance brought them to within five miles of the city.

Square, Moscow, September 1941

PLATE 15

Untitled

Ink, watercolor, and conté on paper
5 1/2 x 7 in. (14 x 17.8 cm)
2013.17.8

The Malyi Theater, which is seen in the background, is among the leading drama theaters in Moscow, while the Bolshoi Theater nearby (the sketch captures the back of the building) houses opera and ballet. Opera, ballet, and theater performances were held in Moscow throughout the war, even at the moments of greatest crisis. Topolski noted color instructions for a later development of the image sketched here.

PLATE 16

Moscow—Listening to the Loudspeakers
[*Listening to the Loudspeaker*]

October 1941
Pen, ink, and watercolor on paper
5 1/2 x 7 in. (14 x 17.8 cm)
2013.17.5

Civilians and soldiers standing on a Moscow street corner listen to the news about developments at the front. Such government-controlled public broadcasts were among the most widespread methods of conveying information to the masses. Loudspeakers were installed on major street corners and in public squares all over the Soviet Union.

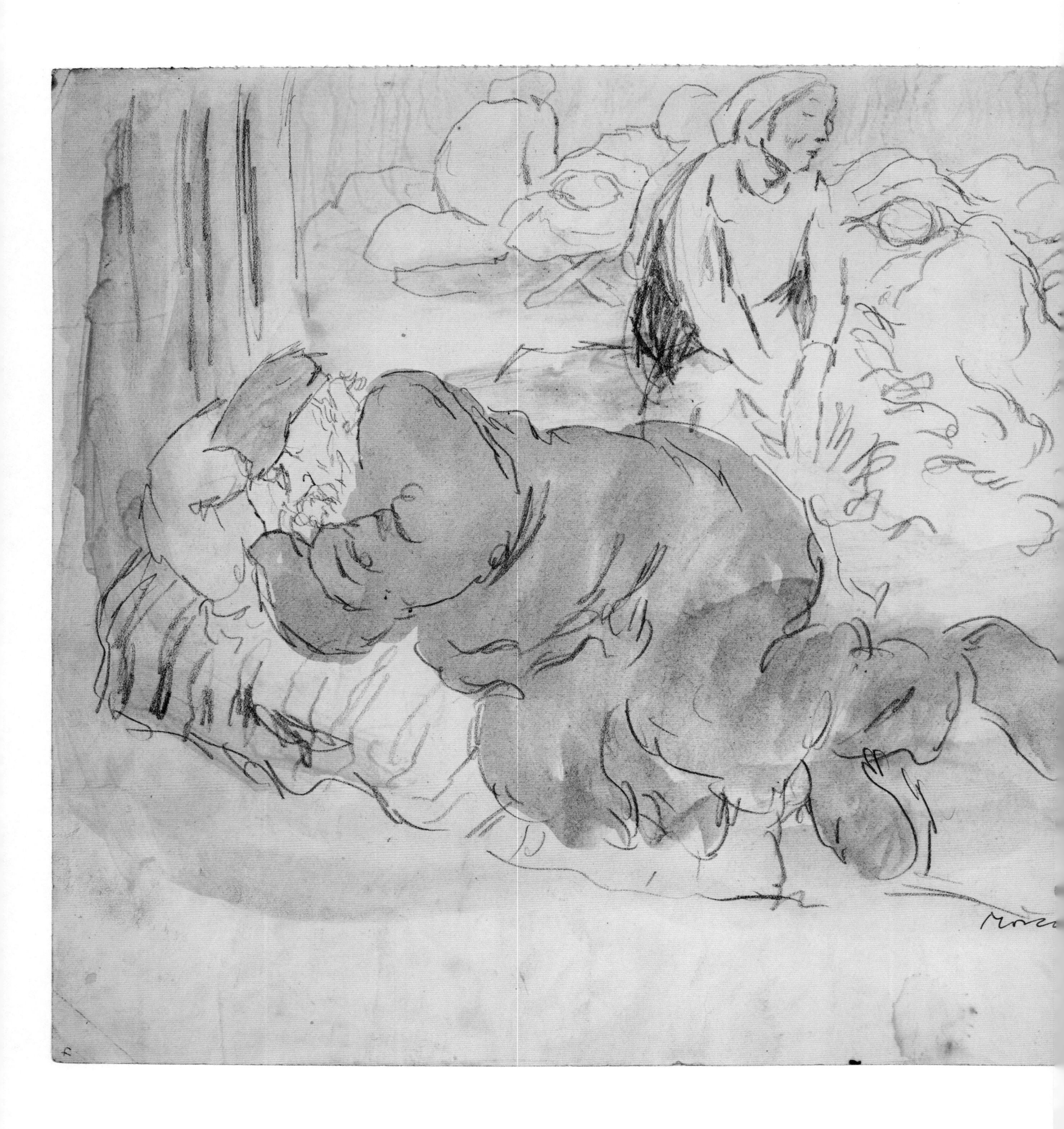

PLATE 17

Moscow Metro
[*In the Underground*]

October 1941
Graphite and ink wash on paper
9 1/2 x 12 5/16 in. (24.1 x 31.3 cm)
2013.17.16

The German air force launched numerous bombing raids on Moscow beginning in summer 1941. During these nights, the Moscow Metro became an air-raid shelter. Topolski had already drawn similar scenes to this in London, during the German air assault on that city.

PLATE 18

Moscow
[*Old people in 'Nikitskie Vorota'*]

Ink on paper
7 x 5 1/2 in. (17.8 x 14 cm)
2013.17.9

Topolski's pen captured elderly people walking by a corner decorated with a patriotic poster proclaiming the invincibility of the Soviet people.

PLATE 19

Young Komsomol (Gen. Zukov's Son)

September 1941
Ink and watercolor on paper
10 x 7 3/8 in. (25.4 x 18.7 cm)
2013.17.11

General Georgii Sergeevich Zhukov (1907–1978) was an officer of the NKVD (People's Commissariat for Internal Affairs) who accompanied Topolski and General Władysław Anders from Moscow to the Polish camp in Buzuluk. His son, sketched here, wears the uniform of the Young Pioneers (red neck scarf, white shirt), an organization that gathered all school children aged ten to fourteen to be indoctrinated in Communist ideology. At age fifteen, adolescents would become members of the Komsomol (Union of Young Communists) until the age of twenty-eight. The Komsomol prepared youth to join the Communist Party.

September 1941. Young Komsomol (gen. Zukov's son)

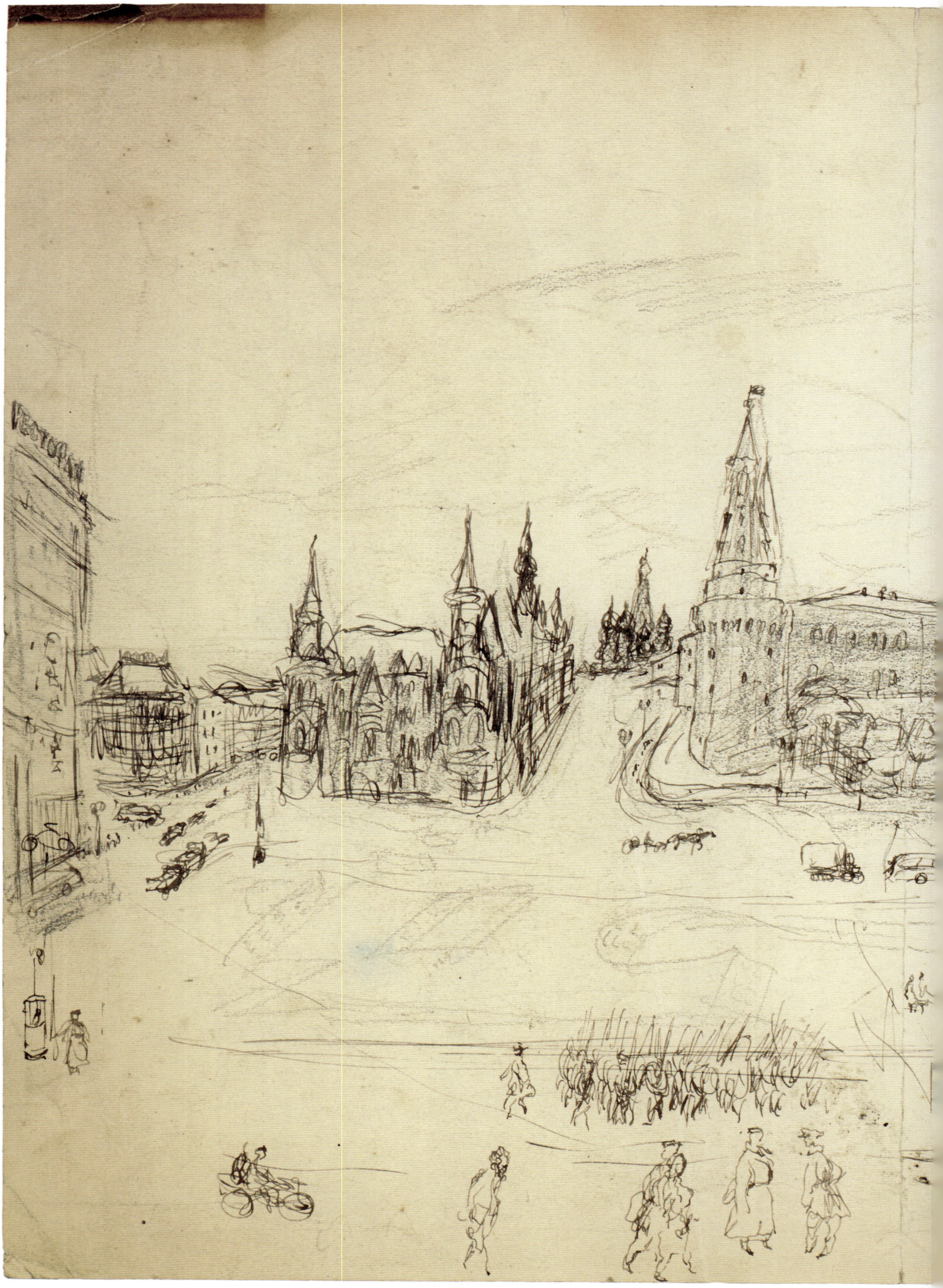

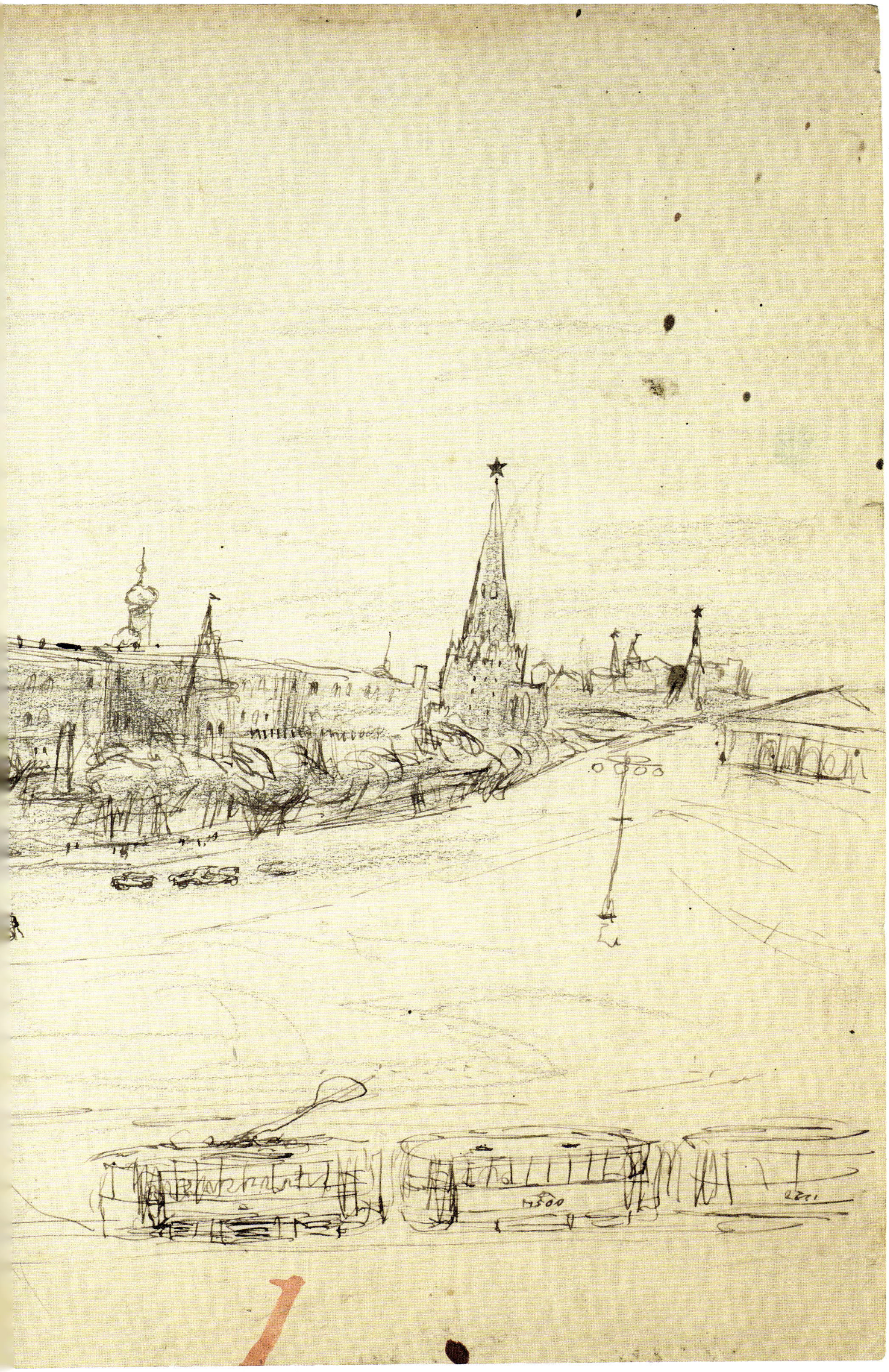

PLATE 20 (previous spread)

Untitled

Pen, ink, and graphite on paper
10 3/4 x 14 3/4 in. (27.3 x 37.5 cm)
2013.17.1

Topolski stayed at the Hotel Natsional while in Moscow. From his window he had a panoramic view of the Kremlin and Red Square, with marching troops joining the traffic in front of the hotel. During the Second World War this elegant pre-revolutionary hotel housed many Allied delegations.

PLATE 21

Shoe Cleaner, Moscow

Ink on paper
5 1/2 x 7 in. (14 x 17.8 cm)
2013.17.17

shoecleaner - Moscow

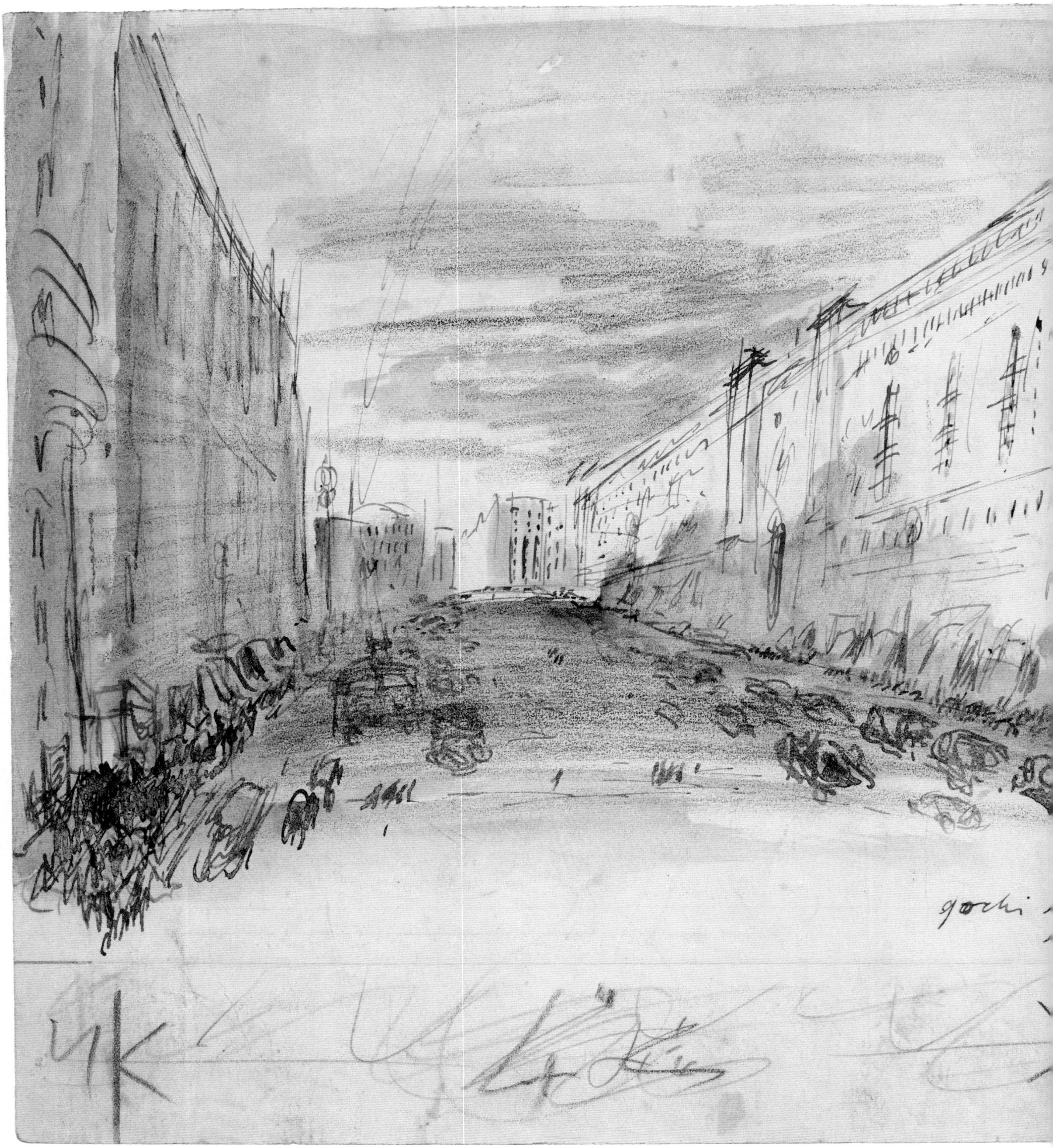

PLATE 22

Gorki Street, Moscow
[*Gorki Street, Formerly Tverskaya*]

September 1941
Pen, ink, watercolor, and graphite on paper
9 3/4 x 12 1/4 in. (24.8 x 32.4 cm)
2013.17.3

This thoroughfare was a symbol of the urban reconstruction that Moscow underwent in the 1930s. All the churches and most other historic buildings were torn down in order to widen the street and replace low-rise buildings with larger apartment blocks and government offices. Today the name of the street has reverted to its pre-Soviet name of Tverskaya.

On a British Cruiser in the Arctic 1941   Fore-control

PLATE 23

On a British Cruiser in the Arctic

Graphite and ink on paper
7 9/16 x 9 15/16 in. (19.2 x 25.2 cm)
2013.17.53

Topolski returned to Britain on board a British cruiser that sailed from Arkhangelsk to Inverness in Scotland. He observed and drew the life of sailors on that mission, whether in combat, relaxing, or on the lookout, as shown in this drawing.

PLATE 24 (following spread)

Untitled

Pen, ink, and graphite on paper
9 15/16 x 7 1/2 in. (25.2 x 19.1 cm)
2013.17.47

PLATE 25 (following spread)

Upper Deck

Graphite and ink on paper
9 15/16 x 7 1/2 in. (25.2 x 19.1 cm)
2013.17.52

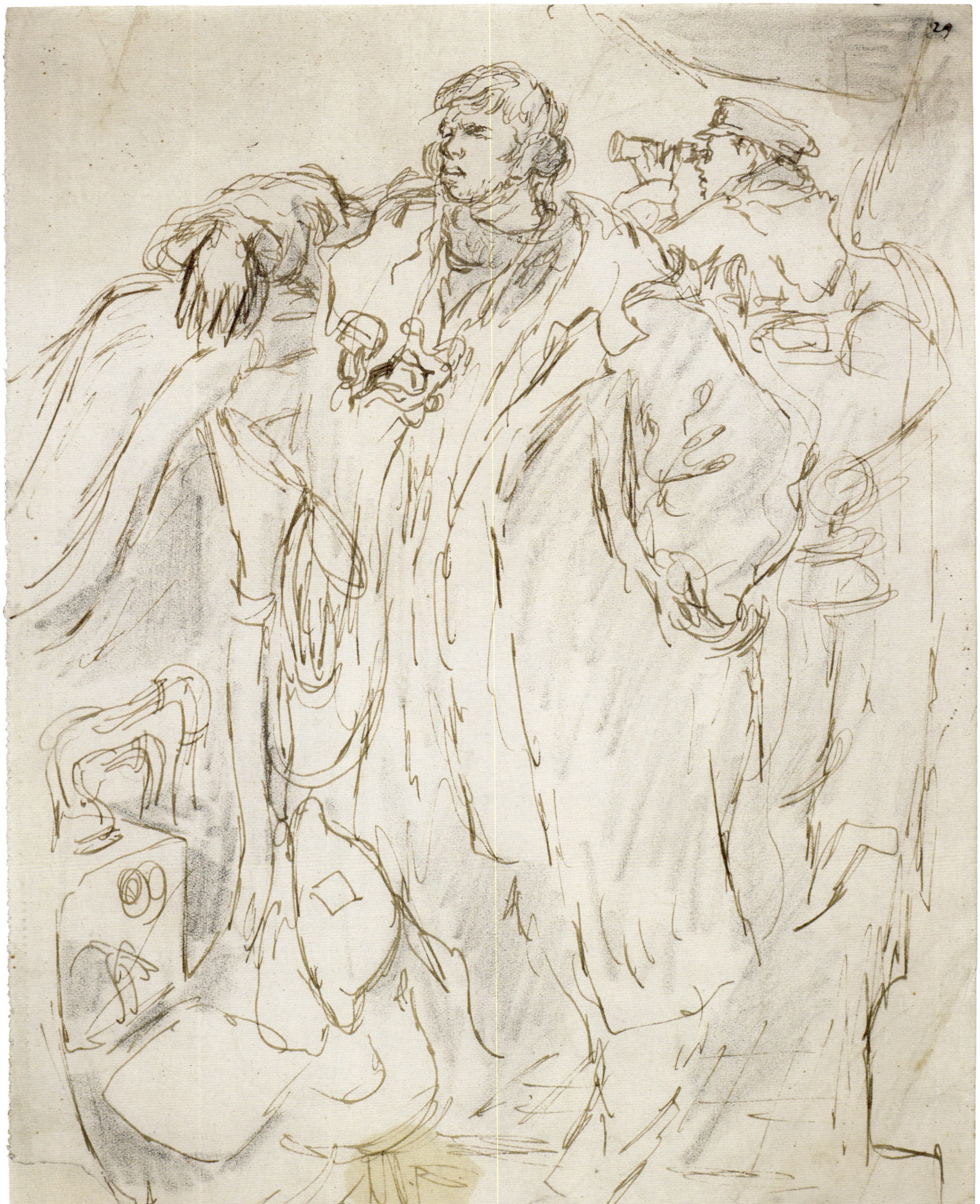

upper-deck

PLATE 26

Quarter-deck

Graphite, ink, and colored pencil on paper
9 15/16 x 7 1/2 in. (25.2 x 19.1)
2013.17.51

Quarter-deck

The Wolfsonian

The Wolfsonian–Florida International University is a museum, library, and research center that uses objects to illustrate the persuasive power of art and design, to explore what it means to be modern, and to tell the story of social, political, and technological changes that have transformed our world. The collections comprise approximately 150,000 objects from the period of 1851 to 1945—the height of the Industrial Revolution to the end of the Second World War—in a variety of media, including fine arts, decorative arts, graphic design, industrial design, architectural drawings, rare publications, and ephemera.